2016 Supervisory Scenarios for Annual Stress Tests Required under the Dodd-Frank Act Stress Testing Rules and the Capital Plan Rule

January 28, 2016

BOARD OF GOVERNORS OF THE FEDERAL RESERVE SYSTEM

Contents

Introduction

The Dodd-Frank Wall Street Reform and Consumer Protection Act requires the Board of Governors of the Federal Reserve System (Board) to conduct an annual supervisory stress test of bank holding companies (BHCs) with $50 billion or greater in total consolidated assets (large BHCs), and to require BHCs and state member banks with total consolidated assets of more than $10 billion to conduct company-run stress tests at least once a year.[1] This publication describes the three supervisory scenarios—baseline, adverse, and severely adverse— that the Board will use in its supervisory stress test for this stress test cycle; that a BHC or state member bank must use in conducting its annual company-run stress test; and that a large BHC must use to estimate projected revenues, losses, reserves, and pro forma capital levels as part of its 2016 capital plan submission.[2] The publication also details additional components that certain BHCs will be required to incorporate into the supervisory scenarios—the global market shock component and the counterparty default component.

---

[1] 12 U.S.C. 5365(i).

[2] See 12 CFR 252.14(b), 12 CFR 252.54(b), and 12 CFR 225.8.

Supervisory Scenarios

The adverse and severely adverse scenarios describe hypothetical sets of conditions designed to assess the strength of banking organizations and their resilience to adverse economic environments. The baseline scenario follows a similar profile to the average projections from a survey of economic forecasters. The scenarios are not forecasts of the Federal Reserve.[3]

The scenarios start in the first quarter of 2016 and extend through the first quarter of 2019. Each scenario includes 28 variables; this set of variables is the same as the set provided in last year's supervisory scenarios. The variables describing economic developments within the United States include:

- **Six measures of economic activity and prices:** percent changes (at an annual rate) in real and nominal gross domestic product (GDP); the unemployment rate of the civilian noninstitutional population aged 16 years and over; percent changes (at an annual rate) in real and nominal disposable personal income; and the percent change (at an annual rate) in the consumer price index (CPI);

- **Four aggregate measures of asset prices or financial conditions:** indexes of house prices, commercial property prices, equity prices, and U.S. stock market volatility; and,

- **Six measures of interest rates:** the rate on the 3-month Treasury bill; the yield on the 5-year Treasury bond; the yield on the 10-year Treasury bond; the yield on a 10-year BBB corporate security; the interest rate associated with a conforming, conventional, fixed-rate 30-year mortgage; and the prime rate.

The variables describing international economic conditions in each scenario include three variables in four countries or country blocks:

- **The three variables for each country or country block:** the percent change (at an annual rate) in real

GDP, the percent change (at an annual rate) in the CPI or local equivalent, and the level of the U.S. dollar/foreign currency exchange rate.

- **The four countries or country blocks included:** the euro area (the 19 European Union member states that have adopted the euro as their common currency), the United Kingdom, developing Asia (the nominal GDP-weighted aggregate of China, India, South Korea, Hong Kong Special Administrative Region, and Taiwan), and Japan.

Baseline, Adverse, and Severely Adverse Scenarios

The following sections describe the baseline scenario, the adverse scenario, and the severely adverse scenario. The variables included in these scenarios are provided in tables at the end of this document. They can also be downloaded as a spreadsheet (together with the historical time series of the variables) from the Board's website, at http://www.federalreserve.gov/bankinforeg/dfa-stress-tests.htm.

Baseline Scenario

The baseline outlook for U.S. real activity, inflation, and interest rates (see Table 1A) is similar to the January 2016 consensus projections from *Blue Chip Economic Indicators*.[4] This scenario does not represent the forecast of the Federal Reserve.

The baseline scenario for the United States is a moderate economic expansion through the projection period. Real GDP grows at an average rate of 2½ percent per year. The unemployment rate declines to 4½ percent in the middle of 2017 and remains near that level through the end of the scenario period. CPI inflation rises to 2½ percent at an annual rate by the middle of 2017 before dropping back to

---

[3] For more on the Federal Reserve's framework for designing scenarios for stress testing, see 12 CFR 252, appendix A.

[4] See Wolters Kluwer Legal and Regulatory Solutions (2016), "Blue Chip Economic Indicators," vol. 41, no. 1 (January 10).

about 2 percent in the first quarter of 2018 and remaining near that level thereafter.

Accompanying the moderate economic expansion, Treasury yields are assumed to rise steadily across the maturity spectrum. Short-term Treasury rates increase from about ½ percent at the beginning of 2016 to about 2¾ percent by the beginning of 2019, while the yields on 10-year Treasury securities rise from 2½ percent to about 3¾ percent over the same period. The prime rate increases in line with short-term Treasury rates and mortgage rates rise in line with long-term Treasury rates. Reflecting strengthening economic conditions, spreads between yields on investment-grade corporate bonds and yields on long-term Treasury securities narrow modestly over the scenario period. Equity prices rise an average of about 4¾ percent per year and equity market volatility is assumed to remain near its historical average level. Nominal house prices rise an average of 2¾ percent per year and commercial real estate prices rise an average of 4¼ percent per year.

The outlook for international variables (see Table 1B) is similar to that reported in the January 2016 *Blue Chip Economic Indicators* and the International Monetary Fund's October 2015 *World Economic Outlook*.[5] The baseline scenario features an expansion in international economic activity, albeit one that proceeds at different rates in the four countries or country blocks under consideration. Real GDP growth in developing Asia averages 6 percent per year over the scenario period; real GDP growth in the United Kingdom averages 2¼ percent per year; and real GDP growth in the euro area and Japan averages 1¾ percent per year and 1 percent per year, respectively.

Adverse Scenario

The adverse scenario is characterized by weakening economic activity across all countries or country blocks included in the scenario. The economic downturn is accompanied by a period of deflation in the United States and in the other countries and country blocks. It is important to note that this is a hypothetical scenario designed to assess the strength of banking organizations and their resilience to adverse economic conditions. This scenario does not represent a forecast of the Federal Reserve.

The adverse scenario features a moderate U.S. recession that begins in the first quarter of 2016 (see Table 2A). Real GDP in the United States falls 1¾ percent from the pre-recession peak in the fourth quarter of 2015 to the recession trough in the first quarter of 2017, while the unemployment rate rises steadily, peaking at 7½ percent in the middle of 2017. The U.S. recession is accompanied by a mild deflationary period, with consumer prices falling about ½ percent over the four quarters of 2016.

Reflecting weak economic conditions and deflationary pressures, short-term interest rates in the United States remain near zero over the projection period. The 10-year Treasury yield declines to 1¼ percent in early 2016 before rising gradually thereafter to 3 percent in the first quarter of 2019. Financial conditions tighten for corporations and households during the recession, with spreads between investment-grade corporate bond yields and 10-year Treasury yields and spreads between mortgage rates and 10-year Treasury yields widening through the end of 2016.

Asset prices decline in the adverse scenario. Equity prices fall approximately 25 percent through the fourth quarter of 2016, accompanied by a moderate rise in equity market volatility. Aggregate house prices and commercial real estate prices experience moderate declines; commercial real estate prices fall 12 percent through the third quarter of 2017 and house prices fall 12 percent through the third quarter of 2018.

Following the end of the recession in the United States, real activity picks up slowly at first and then gains speed; real U.S. GDP growth rises from 1¼ percent at an annual rate in the second quarter of 2017 to 3 percent at an annual rate by the middle of 2018. The unemployment rate declines modestly, to about 7 percent by the end of the scenario period. Consumer prices begin to rise slowly in the first quarter of 2017 and inflation remains subdued through the end of the scenario window. Consumer price inflation reaches 1¾ percent at an annual rate in the first quarter of 2019.

Outside of the United States, the adverse scenario features moderate recessions in the euro area, the United Kingdom, and Japan, as well as below-trend growth in developing Asia (see Table 2B). Weakness in global demand results in deflation across all of the foreign economies under consideration as well as a broad-based decline in commodity prices. Headline consumer prices decline modestly through the end of

---

5   See International Monetary Fund (2015), "World Economic Outlook," www.imf.org/external/pubs/ft/weo/2015/02.

2016 in the euro area and the United Kingdom, and decline through the middle of 2017 in developing Asia. Japan experiences a sharper and more prolonged deflationary period, with prices falling through the second quarter of 2018. The U.S. dollar appreciates relative to the currencies of the countries and country blocks under consideration, reflecting flight-to-safety capital flows; the dollar appreciates most strongly against the euro and the currencies of developing Asia.

Comparison of 2015 Adverse Scenario and 2016 Adverse Scenario

The main difference relative to the 2015 adverse scenario is that this year's adverse scenario features a decline in the CPI—i.e., deflation—in the United States. Deflation in the euro area and Japan was featured as a component of the 2015 adverse scenario, but that scenario also featured a considerable rise in headline U.S. inflation. In this year's adverse scenario, U.S. deflation implies substantially different paths of U.S. Treasury yields relative to the paths in last year's scenario. In this year's scenario, the yield curve is lower and initially flatter than under baseline assumptions, but then steepens over the scenario period. In last year's scenario, by contrast, the yield curve was higher and flatter than under baseline assumptions.

Compared with the 2015 adverse scenario, the period of U.S. deflation that is featured in the 2016 adverse scenario may be expected to reduce nominal household income growth and raise real effective interest rates. These are conditions that may be expected to reduce loan repayments and increase credit losses. The lower path of Treasury rates may be expected to reduce pre-provision net revenue (PPNR), largely through reduced net interest income. However, in addition to these scenario changes, the Federal Reserve's supervisory stress test projections will also reflect changes in the structure, business focus, and recent performance of the BHCs participating in the exercise.

Additional Key Features of the Adverse Scenario

As in last year's adverse scenario, the slowdown in euro area economic activity should be interpreted as a broad-based contraction in euro area demand, not as a contraction that is concentrated in a few specific economies. In addition, the slowdown in developing Asia should be interpreted as a weakening in eco-

nomic conditions across emerging market economies and not merely as a weakening in Asia-specific conditions. Declines in aggregate U.S. real estate prices should be assumed to be concentrated in regions that have experienced rapid price gains over the past several years. Declines in prices of U.S. housing and commercial real estate should also be assumed to be representative of risks to house prices and commercial real estate prices in foreign regions and economies that have experienced rapid price gains over the past several years.

Severely Adverse Scenario

The severely adverse scenario is characterized by a severe global recession, accompanied by a period of heightened corporate financial stress and negative yields for short-term U.S. Treasury securities. It is important to note that this is a hypothetical scenario designed to assess the strength of banking organizations and their resilience to unfavorable economic conditions. This scenario does not represent a forecast of the Federal Reserve.

In this scenario, the level of U.S. real GDP begins to decline in the first quarter of 2016 and reaches a trough in the first quarter of 2017 that is 6¼ percent below the pre-recession peak (see Table 3A). The unemployment rate increases by 5 percentage points, to 10 percent, by the middle of 2017 and headline consumer price inflation rises from about ¼ percent at an annual rate in the first quarter of 2016 to about 1¼ percent at an annual rate by the end of the recession.

Asset prices drop sharply in the scenario, consistent with the developments described above. Equity prices fall approximately 50 percent through the end of 2016, accompanied by a surge in equity market volatility, which approaches the levels attained in 2008. House prices and commercial real estate prices also experience considerable declines, with house prices dropping 25 percent through the third quarter of 2018 and commercial real estate prices falling 30 percent through the second quarter of 2018. Corporate financial conditions are stressed severely, reflecting mounting credit losses, heightened investor risk aversion, and strained market liquidity conditions; the spread between yields on investment-grade corporate bonds and yields on long-term Treasury securities increases to 5¾ percent by the end of 2016.

As a result of the severe decline in real activity and subdued inflation, short-term Treasury rates fall to negative ½ percent by mid-2016 and remain at that level through the end of the scenario. For the purposes of this scenario, it is assumed that the adjustment to negative short-term interest rates proceeds with no additional financial market disruptions. The 10-year Treasury yield drops to about ¼ percent in the first quarter of 2016, rising gradually thereafter to reach about ¾ percent by the end of the recession in early 2017 and about 1¾ percent by the first quarter of 2019.

The international component of this scenario features severe recessions in the euro area, the United Kingdom, and Japan, and a mild recession in developing Asia (see Table 3B). As a result of acute economic weakness, all foreign economies included in the scenario experience a pronounced decline in consumer prices. Reflecting flight-to-safety capital flows during weak economic conditions, the U.S. dollar is assumed to appreciate against the euro, the pound sterling, and the currencies of developing Asia. The dollar is assumed to depreciate modestly against the yen, also in line with flight-to-safety capital flows.

Comparison of 2015 Severely Adverse Scenario and 2016 Severely Adverse Scenario

This year's severely adverse scenario features a more severe downturn in the U.S. economy as compared to last year's scenario. This increase in severity reflects the Federal Reserve's scenario design framework for stress testing, which includes countercyclical elements.[6] Under this framework, the unemployment rate in the severely adverse scenario will reach a peak of at least 10 percent, which leads to a progressively greater increase in the unemployment rate if the starting unemployment rate is below 6 percent. In line with the more severe U.S. recession, this year's severely adverse scenario also features a path of negative short-term U.S. Treasury rates. Furthermore, this year's scenario does not feature the pronounced increase in inflation that was featured in last year's scenario.

Compared with the 2015 severely adverse scenario, weaker economic conditions in the 2016 severely adverse scenario may be expected to result in higher

_____
[6] See 12 CFR 252, appendix A.

credit losses on a wide range of loans and securities. Lower interest rates on Treasury securities suggest larger gains on the existing portfolio of these securities. Negative short-term interest rates may be expected to reduce banks' net interest margins and ultimately, to lower PPNR. However, in addition to these scenario changes, the Federal Reserve's supervisory stress test projections will also reflect changes in the structure, business focus, and recent performance of the BHCs participating in the exercise.

Additional Key Features of the Severely Adverse Scenario

As in the adverse scenario, the weakness in euro area economic conditions should be interpreted as a broad-based contraction in euro area demand, although the impact of this contraction should be assumed to be more protracted in countries with little room for fiscal policy intervention. The sharp slowdown in developing Asia is distributed unevenly across countries, with decelerations more pronounced in the larger economies. Economic conditions in developing Asia should be assumed to be representative of conditions across emerging market economies. In Europe as well as in emerging markets, the economic downturn heightens investor concerns about credit risk for countries with high levels of public debt. Spreads on credit default swaps for these countries increase by magnitudes in line with those experienced by Italy, Portugal, and Spain during 2011 and by emerging markets in 2008.

Declines in aggregate U.S. commercial and residential real estate prices should be assumed to be concentrated in regions that have experienced rapid price gains over the past several years. Declines in prices of U.S. housing and commercial real estate should also be assumed to be representative of risks to house prices and commercial real estate prices in foreign regions and economies, particularly where real estate prices have been growing at a fast clip. Domestically, credit losses on commercial real estate loans backing commercial mortgage-backed securities are greater than would be expected given the general economic and financial stress in the scenario, prompting widespread investor pull-back. Spreads on commercial mortgage-backed securities widen to attain the same peaks reached in the 2007–2009 recession.

Global Market Shock Components for Supervisory Adverse and Severely Adverse Scenarios

The global market shock is a set of instantaneous, hypothetical shocks to a large set of risk factors. Generally, these shocks involve large and sudden changes in asset prices, interest rates, and spreads, reflecting general market distress and heightened uncertainty.[7] BHCs with significant trading activity will be required to include the global market shock as part of their supervisory adverse and severely adverse scenarios.[8] In addition, as discussed below, certain large and highly interconnected BHCs must apply the same global market shock to their counterparty exposures to project losses under the counterparty default scenario component.

The as-of date for the global market shock is January 4, 2016.[9]

2016 Severely Adverse Scenario

The severely adverse scenario's global market shock is designed around three main elements: a sudden sharp increase in general risk premiums and credit risk; significant market illiquidity; and the distress of one or more large entities that rapidly sell a variety of assets into an already fragile market. Liquidity deterioration is most severe in those asset markets that are typically less liquid, such as corporate debt and private equity markets, and is less pronounced in those markets that are typically more liquid such as publicly traded equity and U.S. Treasury markets. Markets facing a significant deterioration in liquidity experience conditions that are generally comparable to the peak-to-trough changes in asset valuations during the 2007–2009 period. The severity of deterioration reflects the market conditions that could occur in the event of a significant pullback in market

liquidity in which market participants are less able to engage in market transactions that could offset and moderate the price dislocations. Declines in markets less affected by the deterioration in liquidity conditions are generally comparable to those experienced in the second half of 2008.

Worsening liquidity also leads prices of related assets that would ordinarily be expected to move together to diverge markedly. In particular, the valuation of certain cash market securities and their derivative counterparts—so-called basis spreads—fail to move together because the normal market mechanics that would ordinarily result in small pricing differentials are impeded by a lack of market liquidity. Notably, option-adjusted spreads on agency mortgage-backed securities (MBS) increase significantly. Illiquidity driven dislocations between the cash and to-be-announced (TBA) forward markets result in larger increases in the option adjusted spreads on securities than in the TBA market. Similarly, relationships between the prices of other financial assets that would normally be expected to move together come under pressure and are weakened. As a result, certain hedging strategies are less effective and resulting losses are larger.

Globally, government bond yield curves undergo marked shifts in level and shape due to market participants' increased risk aversion. The flight-to-quality and lack of liquidity in affected markets pushes risk-free rates down across the term structure in the United States, with some short-term rates dropping below zero. The yield curves for government bonds flatten or invert across Europe and Asia while volatility increases across the term structure. The potential for a prolonged and more acute recession in Europe drive up sovereign credit spreads in the euro zone periphery in a manner generally consistent with the experience of 2011. Emerging market countries with deteriorating economic and fiscal accounts would also experience a sharp increase in sovereign spreads.

The major differences between the 2016 and 2015 severely adverse scenarios include (1) a larger widening in credit spreads for municipal, sovereign, and advanced economies' corporate products; (2) generally, greater declines in the value of private equity investments, recently issued securitized products, and non-agency residential MBS; (3) a more severe widening in basis spreads between closely related assets such as agency MBS and TBA forwards as well as corporate bonds and credit default swaps; and (4) a

---

[7] The global market shock components consist of shocks to a large number of risk factors that include a wide range of financial market variables that affect asset prices, such as a credit spread or the yield on a bond, and, also include, in some cases, shocks to the value of the position itself (for example, the market value of private-equity positions).

[8] For this cycle, six BHCs are subject to the global market shock components: Bank of America Corporation; Citigroup Inc.; The Goldman Sachs Group, Inc.; JPMorgan Chase & Co.; Morgan Stanley; and Wells Fargo & Company. See 12 CFR 252.54(b)(2)(i)

[9] A BHC may use data as of the date that corresponds to its weekly internal risk reporting cycle as long as it falls during the business of the as-of date for the global market shock (i.e., January 4, 2016 to January 8, 2016).

general decline in U.S. Treasury rates, resulting in negative short-term rates, while short-term government rates in Europe rise to positive or slightly negative levels, and Asian government rates across the term structure flatten or invert. These differences are intended to reflect the result of a more significant drop in liquidity than was assumed in the 2015 severely adverse scenario and would be expected to result in notably higher losses on more illiquid assets.

2016 Adverse Scenario

The global market shock component for the adverse scenario simulates an extended low-growth environment and muted market volatility across most asset classes and term structures. Domestic interest rates move lower, particularly for longer-maturity securities, with lower volatility. Due to reduced demand, global commodity prices decline moderately. MBS and credit spreads widen moderately. Internationally, yield curves move lower and flatten while sovereign credit spreads widen moderately. Select currency markets also experience small flight-to-quality moves. Equity markets experience a mild correction with a measured increase in volatility.

The major difference between the 2016 and 2015 adverse scenarios is the addition of elements that are distinct from and not mechanically linked to the severely adverse scenario. In particular, compared to 2015, the 2016 adverse scenario includes (1) more muted changes in price, spread, and volatility levels across most markets; and (2) a general decline in U.S. Treasury rates, with short-term government rates in most other countries and regions rising in the short term and declining in the longer term.

Counterparty Default Component for Supervisory Adverse and Severely Adverse Scenarios

In CCAR 2016, the eight BHCs with substantial trading or custodial operations will be required to

incorporate a counterparty default scenario component into their supervisory adverse and severely adverse stress scenarios.[10] In connection with the counterparty default scenario component, these BHCs will be required to estimate and report the potential losses and related effects on capital associated with the instantaneous and unexpected default of the counterparty that would generate the largest losses across their derivatives and securities financing activities, including securities lending, and repurchase or reverse repurchase agreement activities. The counterparty default scenario component is an add-on to the macroeconomic conditions and financial market environment specified in the Federal Reserve's adverse and severely adverse stress scenarios.

The counterparty default scenario component involves the instantaneous and unexpected default of the BHC's largest counterparty.[11] Each BHC's largest counterparty will be determined by net stressed losses; estimated by applying the global market shock to revalue non-cash securities financing activity assets (securities or collateral) posted or received; and for derivatives, to the value of the trade position and non-cash collateral exchanged. The as-of date for the counterparty default scenario component is January 4, 2016—the same date as the global market shock.[12]

---

[10] The eight BHCs subject to the counterparty default component are as follows: Bank of America Corporation; The Bank of New York Mellon Corp.; Citigroup Inc.; The Goldman Sachs Group, Inc.; JPMorgan Chase & Co.; Morgan Stanley; State Street Corp.; and Wells Fargo & Company. See 12 CFR 252.54(b)(2)(ii).

[11] In selecting its largest counterparty, a BHC will not consider certain sovereign entities (Canada, France, Germany, Italy, Japan, the United Kingdom, and the United States) or designated central clearing counterparties.

[12] As with the global market shock, a BHC may use data as of the date that corresponds to its weekly internal risk reporting cycle as long as it falls during the business week of the as-of date for the counterparty default scenario component (i.e., January 4 to January 8, 2016).

Variables Considered in Scenarios

Table 1A. Supervisory baseline scenario: Domestic, Q1:2001Q1:2019
Percent unless otherwise indicated

Date	Real GDP growth	Nominal GDP growth	Real disposable income growth	Nominal disposable income growth	Unemployment rate	CPI inflation rate	3-month Treasury rate	5-year Treasury yield	10-year Treasury yield	BBB corporate yield	Mortgage rate	Prime rate	Dow Jones Total Stock Market Index	House Price Index	Commercial Real Estate Price Index	Market Volatility Index
													Level			
Q1 2001	-1.1	1.4	3.5	6.3	4.2	3.9	4.8	4.9	5.3	7.4	7.0	8.6	10,645.9	113.3	139.0	32.8
Q2 2001	2.1	5.1	-0.3	1.6	4.4	2.8	3.7	4.9	5.5	7.5	7.1	7.3	11,407.2	115.2	139.0	34.7
Q3 2001	-1.3	0.0	9.8	10.1	4.8	1.1	3.2	4.6	5.3	7.3	6.9	6.6	9,563.0	117.5	141.0	43.7
Q4 2001	1.1	2.3	-4.9	-4.6	5.5	-0.3	1.9	4.2	5.1	7.2	6.8	5.2	10,707.7	119.8	136.0	35.3
Q1 2002	3.7	5.1	10.1	10.9	5.7	1.3	1.7	4.5	5.4	7.6	7.0	4.8	10,775.7	122.1	137.0	26.1
Q2 2002	2.2	3.8	2.0	5.2	5.8	3.2	1.7	4.5	5.4	7.6	6.8	4.8	9,384.0	125.4	136.0	28.4
Q3 2002	2.0	3.8	-0.5	1.5	5.7	2.2	1.6	3.4	4.5	7.3	6.2	4.8	7,773.6	128.6	139.0	45.1
Q4 2002	0.3	2.4	1.9	3.8	5.9	2.4	1.3	3.1	4.3	7.0	6.1	4.5	8,343.2	131.3	142.0	42.6
Q1 2003	2.1	4.6	1.1	4.0	5.9	4.2	1.2	2.9	4.2	6.5	5.8	4.3	8,051.9	134.1	148.0	34.7
Q2 2003	3.8	5.1	5.9	6.3	6.1	-0.7	1.0	2.6	3.8	5.7	5.5	4.2	9,342.4	137.0	149.0	29.1
Q3 2003	6.9	9.3	6.7	9.3	6.1	3.0	0.9	3.1	4.4	6.0	6.1	4.0	9,649.7	141.0	147.0	22.7
Q4 2003	4.8	6.8	1.6	3.3	5.8	1.5	0.9	3.2	4.4	5.8	5.9	4.0	10,799.6	145.9	146.0	21.1
Q1 2004	2.3	5.9	2.9	6.1	5.7	3.4	0.9	3.0	4.1	5.5	5.6	4.0	11,039.4	151.6	153.0	21.6
Q2 2004	3.0	6.6	4.0	7.0	5.6	3.2	1.1	3.7	4.7	6.1	6.2	4.0	11,144.6	157.9	160.0	20.0
Q3 2004	3.7	6.3	2.1	4.5	5.4	2.6	1.5	3.5	4.4	5.8	5.9	4.4	10,893.8	163.2	172.0	19.3
Q4 2004	3.5	6.4	5.1	8.5	5.4	4.4	2.0	3.5	4.3	5.4	5.7	4.9	11,951.5	169.2	176.0	16.6
Q1 2005	4.3	8.3	-3.8	-1.8	5.3	2.0	2.5	3.9	4.4	5.4	5.8	5.4	11,637.3	177.1	176.0	14.6
Q2 2005	2.1	5.1	3.2	6.0	5.1	2.7	2.9	3.9	4.2	5.5	5.7	5.9	11,856.7	184.5	182.0	17.7
Q3 2005	3.4	7.3	2.1	6.6	5.0	6.2	3.4	4.0	4.3	5.5	5.8	6.4	12,282.9	190.2	187.0	14.2
Q4 2005	2.3	5.4	3.4	6.6	5.0	3.8	3.8	4.4	4.6	5.9	6.2	7.0	12,497.2	194.8	195.0	16.5
Q1 2006	4.9	8.2	9.5	11.5	4.7	2.1	4.4	4.6	4.7	6.0	6.3	7.4	13,121.6	198.0	200.0	14.6
Q2 2006	1.2	4.5	0.6	3.7	4.6	3.7	4.7	5.0	5.2	6.5	6.6	7.9	12,808.9	197.1	209.0	23.8
Q3 2006	0.4	3.2	1.2	4.1	4.6	3.8	4.9	4.8	5.0	6.4	6.5	8.3	13,322.5	195.8	219.0	18.6
Q4 2006	3.2	4.6	5.3	4.6	4.4	-1.6	4.9	4.6	4.7	6.1	6.2	8.3	14,215.8	195.8	217.0	12.7
Q1 2007	0.2	4.8	2.6	6.5	4.5	4.0	5.0	4.6	4.8	6.1	6.2	8.3	14,354.0	193.3	227.0	19.6
Q2 2007	3.1	5.4	0.8	4.0	4.5	4.6	4.7	4.7	4.9	6.3	6.4	8.3	15,163.1	188.5	236.0	18.9
Q3 2007	2.7	4.2	1.1	3.4	4.7	2.6	4.3	4.5	4.8	6.5	6.5	8.2	15,317.8	183.2	249.0	30.8
Q4 2007	1.4	3.2	0.3	4.4	4.8	5.0	3.4	3.8	4.4	6.4	6.2	7.5	14,753.6	177.8	251.0	31.1
Q1 2008	-2.7	-0.5	2.9	6.5	5.0	4.4	2.1	2.8	3.9	6.5	5.9	6.2	13,284.1	171.1	240.0	32.2
Q2 2008	2.0	4.0	8.7	13.3	5.3	5.3	1.6	3.2	4.1	6.8	6.1	5.1	13,016.4	163.9	224.0	24.1
Q3 2008	-1.9	0.8	-8.9	-5.1	6.0	6.3	1.5	3.1	4.1	7.2	6.3	5.0	11,826.0	157.4	233.0	46.7
Q4 2008	-8.2	-7.7	2.6	-3.2	6.9	-8.9	0.3	2.2	3.7	9.4	5.8	4.1	9,056.7	149.5	223.0	80.9
Q1 2009	-5.4	-4.5	-0.8	-3.0	8.3	-2.7	0.2	1.9	3.2	9.0	5.0	3.3	8,044.2	143.5	209.0	56.7
Q2 2009	-0.5	-1.2	2.9	4.7	9.3	2.1	0.2	2.3	3.7	8.2	5.1	3.3	9,342.8	143.2	178.0	42.3
Q3 2009	1.3	1.2	-4.3	-1.9	9.6	3.5	0.2	2.5	3.8	6.8	5.1	3.3	10,812.8	144.3	154.0	31.3
Q4 2009	3.9	5.2	-0.5	2.2	9.9	3.2	0.1	2.3	3.7	6.1	4.9	3.3	11,385.1	145.2	155.0	30.7
Q1 2010	1.7	3.2	0.4	1.8	9.8	0.6	0.1	2.4	3.9	5.8	5.0	3.3	12,032.5	145.5	150.0	27.3
Q2 2010	3.9	5.8	5.3	5.8	9.6	-0.1	0.1	2.3	3.6	5.6	4.8	3.3	10,645.8	144.4	165.0	45.8
Q3 2010	2.7	4.6	2.0	3.2	9.5	1.2	0.2	1.6	2.9	5.1	4.4	3.3	11,814.0	141.6	167.0	32.9

(continued on next page)

Table 1A.—continued

Date	Real GDP growth	Nominal GDP growth	Real dispo-sable income growth	Nominal dispo-sable income growth	Unem-ployment rate	CPI inflation rate	3-month Treasury rate	5-year Treasury yield	10-year Treasury yield	BBB corporate yield	Mortgage rate	Prime rate	Level			
													Dow Jones Total Stock Market Index	House Price Index	Com-mercial Real Estate Price Index	Market Volatility Index
Q4 2010	2.5	4.7	2.8	5.0	9.5	3.3	0.1	1.5	3.0	5.0	4.5	3.3	13,131.5	140.3	173.0	23.5
Q1 2011	-1.5	0.2	5.0	8.2	9.1	4.3	0.1	2.1	3.5	5.4	4.9	3.3	13,908.5	138.5	180.0	29.4
Q2 2011	2.9	6.0	-0.6	3.5	9.1	4.7	0.0	1.8	3.3	5.1	4.6	3.3	13,843.5	137.7	177.0	22.7
Q3 2011	0.8	3.3	2.1	4.3	9.0	2.6	0.0	1.1	2.5	4.9	4.2	3.3	11,676.5	137.7	177.0	48.0
Q4 2011	4.6	5.2	0.2	1.6	8.6	1.7	0.0	1.0	2.1	5.0	4.0	3.3	13,019.3	137.6	188.0	45.5
Q1 2012	2.7	4.9	6.7	9.2	8.3	2.2	0.1	0.9	2.1	4.7	3.9	3.3	14,627.5	139.6	188.0	23.0
Q2 2012	1.9	3.8	3.1	4.4	8.2	1.0	0.1	0.8	1.8	4.5	3.8	3.3	14,100.2	142.8	189.0	26.7
Q3 2012	0.5	2.7	-0.2	1.1	8.0	1.8	0.1	0.7	1.6	4.2	3.5	3.3	14,894.7	145.7	197.0	20.5
Q4 2012	0.1	1.7	10.9	13.3	7.8	2.6	0.1	0.7	1.7	3.9	3.4	3.3	14,834.9	149.3	198.0	22.7
Q1 2013	1.9	3.6	-15.9	-14.7	7.7	1.4	0.1	0.8	1.9	4.0	3.5	3.3	16,396.2	153.8	202.0	19.0
Q2 2013	1.1	2.1	2.7	3.1	7.5	-0.1	0.1	0.9	2.0	4.1	3.7	3.3	16,771.3	158.8	213.0	20.5
Q3 2013	3.0	4.9	2.2	3.9	7.2	2.3	0.0	1.5	2.7	4.9	4.4	3.3	17,718.3	163.0	224.0	17.0
Q4 2013	3.8	5.6	0.6	2.0	7.0	1.4	0.1	1.4	2.8	4.8	4.3	3.3	19,413.2	166.3	229.0	20.3
Q1 2014	-0.9	0.6	4.0	5.6	6.7	2.1	0.0	1.6	2.8	4.6	4.4	3.3	19,711.2	169.3	230.0	21.4
Q2 2014	4.6	6.9	3.0	5.2	6.2	2.4	0.0	1.7	2.7	4.3	4.2	3.3	20,568.7	170.7	239.0	17.0
Q3 2014	4.3	6.0	2.7	3.9	6.1	1.2	0.0	1.7	2.5	4.2	4.1	3.3	20,458.8	172.5	245.0	17.0
Q4 2014	2.1	2.2	4.7	4.2	5.7	-0.9	0.0	1.6	2.3	4.2	3.9	3.3	21,424.6	174.5	252.0	26.3
Q1 2015	0.6	0.8	3.9	1.9	5.6	-3.1	0.0	1.5	2.0	4.0	3.7	3.3	21,707.6	177.3	260.0	22.4
Q2 2015	3.9	6.1	2.6	4.9	5.4	3.0	0.0	1.5	2.2	4.2	3.8	3.3	21,630.9	179.4	264.0	18.9
Q3 2015	2.0	3.3	3.8	5.1	5.2	1.6	0.0	1.6	2.3	4.5	3.9	3.3	19,959.3	181.7	270.0	40.7
Q4 2015	1.9	1.9	3.5	3.8	5.0	0.2	0.1	1.6	2.2	4.6	3.9	3.3	21,100.9	183.1	273.4	24.4
Q1 2016	2.5	4.0	2.8	3.5	4.9	1.2	0.4	1.8	2.4	4.5	4.1	3.6	21,336.7	184.0	276.8	24.8
Q2 2016	2.6	4.0	2.5	4.3	4.8	2.2	0.6	2.0	2.6	4.7	4.2	3.8	21,578.3	185.2	280.3	24.6
Q3 2016	2.6	4.3	2.6	4.5	4.7	2.3	0.9	2.2	2.7	4.8	4.3	4.0	21,834.8	186.3	283.8	23.2
Q4 2016	2.5	4.3	2.6	4.6	4.6	2.3	1.0	2.4	2.9	4.9	4.5	4.1	22,093.2	187.5	287.4	22.7
Q1 2017	2.4	4.1	2.8	4.8	4.6	2.2	1.3	2.6	3.0	5.0	4.6	4.4	22,347.4	188.7	291.0	22.5
Q2 2017	2.5	4.6	2.6	4.8	4.6	2.4	1.5	2.7	3.1	5.1	4.7	4.6	22,626.3	189.9	294.7	22.0
Q3 2017	2.3	4.6	2.5	4.7	4.5	2.4	1.9	2.9	3.3	5.2	4.9	5.0	22,908.0	191.1	298.4	21.4
Q4 2017	2.3	4.4	2.6	4.7	4.5	2.3	2.2	3.0	3.4	5.3	5.0	5.3	23,183.2	192.2	302.1	21.7
Q1 2018	2.6	4.3	2.9	4.7	4.5	2.0	2.4	3.1	3.5	5.4	5.2	5.5	23,458.2	193.7	304.4	21.4
Q2 2018	2.4	4.2	2.6	4.6	4.6	2.1	2.6	3.2	3.6	5.5	5.3	5.7	23,733.2	195.2	306.7	21.5
Q3 2018	2.3	4.2	2.6	4.5	4.6	2.1	2.7	3.2	3.7	5.6	5.4	5.8	24,008.9	196.6	309.0	21.4
Q4 2018	2.3	4.1	2.5	4.5	4.7	2.1	2.8	3.3	3.8	5.6	5.5	5.9	24,285.1	198.1	311.4	21.5
Q1 2019	2.1	4.0	2.4	4.3	4.7	2.1	2.8	3.4	3.8	5.6	5.5	5.9	24,555.9	199.6	313.7	21.4

Note: Refer to Notes Regarding Scenario Variables for more information on variables.

Table 1B. Supervisory baseline scenario: International, Q1:2001Q1:2019
Percent unless otherwise indicated

Date	Euro area real GDP growth	Euro area inflation	Euro area bilateral dollar exchange rate (USD/euro)	Developing Asia real GDP growth	Developing Asia inflation	Developing Asia bilateral dollar exchange rate (F/USD, index)	Japan real GDP growth	Japan inflation	Japan bilateral dollar exchange rate (yen/USD)	U.K. real GDP growth	U.K. inflation	U.K. bilateral dollar exchange rate (USD/pound)
Q1 2001	3.8	1.1	0.879	5.0	1.7	106.0	2.6	-1.2	125.5	4.6	0.1	1.419
Q2 2001	0.1	4.1	0.847	5.5	2.2	106.1	-0.7	-0.3	124.7	3.1	3.1	1.408
Q3 2001	0.3	1.4	0.910	4.7	1.1	106.4	-4.4	-1.1	119.2	2.6	1.0	1.469
Q4 2001	0.5	1.7	0.890	8.4	0.2	106.9	-0.5	-1.4	131.0	1.4	0.0	1.454
Q1 2002	0.9	3.0	0.872	7.6	0.4	107.3	-0.9	-2.7	132.7	1.6	1.9	1.425
Q2 2002	2.0	2.0	0.986	8.1	1.2	104.8	4.3	1.7	119.9	3.3	0.9	1.525
Q3 2002	1.6	1.6	0.988	7.3	1.3	105.5	2.6	-0.7	121.7	3.9	1.4	1.570
Q4 2002	0.3	2.4	1.049	6.4	0.9	104.5	1.5	-0.4	118.8	3.6	1.9	1.610
Q1 2003	-0.9	3.3	1.090	6.5	3.6	105.5	-2.2	-1.6	118.1	2.9	1.6	1.579
Q2 2003	0.4	0.3	1.150	2.3	1.2	104.0	5.2	1.7	119.9	3.7	0.3	1.653
Q3 2003	2.0	2.2	1.165	14.2	0.0	102.6	1.7	-0.7	111.4	3.1	1.7	1.662
Q4 2003	3.1	2.2	1.260	12.9	5.6	103.4	4.2	-0.6	107.1	3.0	1.7	1.784
Q1 2004	2.0	2.3	1.229	5.5	4.0	101.4	3.8	-0.9	104.2	2.7	1.3	1.840
Q2 2004	2.2	2.4	1.218	7.1	4.1	102.8	0.3	1.1	109.4	2.2	1.0	1.813
Q3 2004	1.3	2.0	1.242	8.2	3.9	102.7	0.6	0.1	110.2	0.9	1.1	1.809
Q4 2004	1.5	2.4	1.354	6.3	0.9	98.9	-1.0	1.7	102.7	1.9	2.4	1.916
Q1 2005	0.6	1.5	1.297	10.3	2.9	98.6	0.8	-2.7	107.2	2.8	2.6	1.889
Q2 2005	2.8	2.2	1.210	8.9	1.5	98.9	5.4	-1.2	110.9	4.4	1.9	1.793
Q3 2005	3.0	3.2	1.206	9.3	2.3	98.6	1.4	-1.3	113.3	4.1	2.7	1.770
Q4 2005	2.4	2.5	1.184	11.6	1.7	98.1	0.7	0.7	117.9	5.9	1.4	1.719
Q1 2006	3.7	1.7	1.214	10.9	2.4	96.8	1.7	1.3	117.5	1.5	1.9	1.739
Q2 2006	4.4	2.5	1.278	7.1	3.2	96.7	1.7	-0.1	114.5	1.2	3.0	1.849
Q3 2006	2.6	2.0	1.269	10.3	2.1	96.4	-0.3	0.5	118.0	0.5	3.3	1.872
Q4 2006	4.4	0.9	1.320	11.1	3.8	94.6	5.2	-0.4	119.0	2.3	2.6	1.959
Q1 2007	3.2	2.2	1.337	13.7	3.6	94.0	4.0	-0.2	117.6	3.9	2.6	1.969
Q2 2007	2.5	2.3	1.352	10.6	4.9	91.9	0.6	0.0	123.4	2.4	1.7	2.006
Q3 2007	2.0	2.1	1.422	8.6	7.4	90.6	-1.5	0.1	115.0	3.1	0.2	2.039
Q4 2007	2.0	4.9	1.460	12.9	6.1	89.4	3.4	2.2	111.7	3.1	4.0	1.984
Q1 2008	2.3	4.2	1.581	7.1	8.1	88.0	2.7	1.3	99.9	1.0	3.7	1.986
Q2 2008	-1.3	3.2	1.575	6.1	6.4	88.7	-4.6	1.6	106.2	-2.2	5.7	1.991
Q3 2008	-2.2	3.2	1.408	3.1	2.8	91.6	-4.1	3.6	105.9	-6.6	5.8	1.780
Q4 2008	-7.1	-1.4	1.392	0.1	-0.9	92.3	-12.5	-2.2	90.8	-8.7	0.5	1.462
Q1 2009	-11.3	-1.1	1.326	3.8	-1.4	94.2	-15.1	-3.6	99.2	-6.1	-0.1	1.430
Q2 2009	-0.8	0.0	1.402	15.4	2.3	92.3	7.1	-1.7	96.4	-0.8	2.2	1.645
Q3 2009	1.2	1.1	1.463	12.6	3.9	91.3	0.4	-1.2	89.5	0.6	3.5	1.600
Q4 2009	2.0	1.6	1.433	9.0	5.2	90.7	7.1	-1.6	93.1	1.4	3.0	1.617
Q1 2010	1.7	1.8	1.353	9.8	4.6	89.8	5.8	0.9	93.4	1.5	4.0	1.519
Q2 2010	3.9	2.0	1.229	9.8	3.4	91.1	4.6	-1.2	88.5	3.3	3.2	1.495
Q3 2010	1.9	1.6	1.360	8.8	3.9	88.4	6.1	-2.1	83.5	2.0	2.3	1.573
Q4 2010	2.1	2.6	1.327	9.3	7.7	87.4	-2.0	1.3	81.7	0.4	4.0	1.539
Q1 2011	3.5	3.6	1.418	9.5	6.3	86.5	-7.7	-0.4	82.8	3.0	6.7	1.605
Q2 2011	0.0	3.2	1.452	7.1	5.4	85.3	-2.2	-0.4	80.6	1.4	4.7	1.607
Q3 2011	-0.1	1.4	1.345	5.9	5.0	87.4	11.2	0.3	77.0	3.3	3.7	1.562
Q4 2011	-1.2	3.5	1.297	6.1	3.4	87.4	0.9	-0.7	77.0	0.6	3.4	1.554
Q1 2012	-0.7	2.7	1.333	7.1	3.2	86.4	3.6	1.9	82.4	0.9	2.1	1.599
Q2 2012	-1.3	2.3	1.267	5.9	4.0	88.1	-1.3	-0.7	79.8	-0.7	2.0	1.569
Q3 2012	-0.6	1.6	1.286	6.5	1.9	86.3	-1.9	-2.1	77.9	4.1	2.3	1.613
Q4 2012	-1.7	2.4	1.319	7.2	3.7	86.0	-0.4	0.0	86.6	-0.2	4.0	1.626
Q1 2013	-1.0	1.1	1.282	6.3	4.2	86.3	4.0	0.4	94.2	2.7	2.9	1.519
Q2 2013	1.6	0.5	1.301	7.0	3.1	87.3	3.1	0.6	99.2	2.4	1.7	1.521
Q3 2013	1.0	1.3	1.354	7.4	3.5	86.8	2.0	2.4	98.3	3.8	2.1	1.618

(continued on next page)

Table 1B.—*continued*

Date	Euro area real GDP growth	Euro area inflation	Euro area bilateral dollar exchange rate (USD/euro)	Developing Asia real GDP growth	Developing Asia inflation	Developing Asia bilateral dollar exchange rate (F/USD, index)	Japan real GDP growth	Japan inflation	Japan bilateral dollar exchange rate (yen/USD)	U.K. real GDP growth	U.K. inflation	U.K. bilateral dollar exchange rate (USD/pound)
Q4 2013	0.8	0.3	1.378	6.5	4.0	85.9	-0.7	2.3	105.3	2.6	1.5	1.657
Q1 2014	0.9	0.6	1.378	5.9	1.5	86.9	5.0	0.7	103.0	2.6	1.8	1.668
Q2 2014	0.2	0.1	1.369	7.0	2.7	86.8	-7.2	9.3	101.3	3.2	1.5	1.711
Q3 2014	1.2	0.3	1.263	7.5	2.2	87.2	-2.8	1.3	109.7	2.6	0.9	1.622
Q4 2014	1.5	-0.4	1.210	5.6	1.0	88.2	1.8	-0.8	119.9	2.7	-0.6	1.558
Q1 2015	2.2	-1.2	1.074	5.8	1.0	88.1	4.4	-0.3	120.0	1.5	-1.2	1.485
Q2 2015	1.6	2.2	1.115	6.2	2.9	88.5	-0.5	1.7	122.1	2.2	0.8	1.573
Q3 2015	1.2	-0.1	1.116	7.0	2.6	91.1	1.0	0.0	119.8	1.8	1.0	1.512
Q4 2015	1.6	-0.1	1.086	6.2	2.3	92.2	1.0	-0.3	120.3	2.4	-0.3	1.475
Q1 2016	1.7	0.9	1.072	6.1	2.3	92.8	1.1	0.7	121.1	2.3	1.1	1.476
Q2 2016	1.8	1.2	1.060	6.0	2.3	93.4	1.1	0.9	122.0	2.1	1.4	1.480
Q3 2016	1.8	1.3	1.051	5.9	2.3	94.0	1.1	1.1	122.8	2.0	1.6	1.487
Q4 2016	1.8	1.4	1.043	5.9	2.4	94.5	1.0	1.4	123.5	2.0	1.8	1.494
Q1 2017	1.8	1.5	1.050	5.9	2.6	94.4	0.8	1.7	123.9	2.2	1.9	1.501
Q2 2017	1.7	1.5	1.058	6.0	2.7	94.2	0.7	1.8	124.1	2.3	1.9	1.507
Q3 2017	1.7	1.6	1.065	6.0	2.8	94.0	0.6	1.8	124.4	2.3	1.9	1.513
Q4 2017	1.7	1.5	1.073	6.0	2.8	93.8	0.7	1.6	124.5	2.3	1.8	1.518
Q1 2018	1.6	1.5	1.079	6.0	2.8	93.7	0.8	1.4	124.0	2.2	1.8	1.521
Q2 2018	1.6	1.5	1.085	6.0	2.9	93.6	0.9	1.2	123.4	2.1	1.7	1.523
Q3 2018	1.6	1.5	1.090	6.0	2.9	93.6	1.0	1.1	122.7	2.1	1.7	1.526
Q4 2018	1.6	1.6	1.095	6.1	3.0	93.5	1.0	1.2	122.0	2.1	1.7	1.528
Q1 2019	1.6	1.6	1.102	6.2	3.2	93.4	1.0	1.3	121.0	2.1	1.7	1.533

Note: **Refer to** Notes Regarding Scenario Variables **for more information on variables.**

Table 2A. Supervisory adverse scenario: Domestic, Q1:2001Q1:2019
Percent unless otherwise indicated

Date	Real GDP growth	Nominal GDP growth	Real disposable income growth	Nominal disposable income growth	Unemployment rate	CPI inflation rate	3-month Treasury rate	5-year Treasury yield	10-year Treasury yield	BBB corporate yield	Mortgage rate	Prime rate	Level			
													Dow Jones Total Stock Market Index	House Price Index	Commercial Real Estate Price Index	Market Volatility Index
Q1 2001	-1.1	1.4	3.5	6.3	4.2	3.9	4.8	4.9	5.3	7.4	7.0	8.6	10,645.9	113.3	139.0	32.8
Q2 2001	2.1	5.1	-0.3	1.6	4.4	2.8	3.7	4.9	5.5	7.5	7.1	7.3	11,407.2	115.2	139.0	34.7
Q3 2001	-1.3	0.0	9.8	10.1	4.8	1.1	3.2	4.6	5.3	7.3	6.9	6.6	9,563.0	117.5	141.0	43.7
Q4 2001	1.1	2.3	-4.9	-4.6	5.5	-0.3	1.9	4.2	5.1	7.2	6.8	5.2	10,707.7	119.8	136.0	35.3
Q1 2002	3.7	5.1	10.1	10.9	5.7	1.3	1.7	4.5	5.4	7.6	7.0	4.8	10,775.7	122.1	137.0	26.1
Q2 2002	2.2	3.8	2.0	5.2	5.8	3.2	1.7	4.5	5.4	7.6	6.8	4.8	9,384.0	125.4	136.0	28.4
Q3 2002	2.0	3.8	-0.5	1.5	5.7	2.2	1.6	3.4	4.5	7.3	6.2	4.8	7,773.6	128.6	139.0	45.1
Q4 2002	0.3	2.4	1.9	3.8	5.9	2.4	1.3	3.1	4.3	7.0	6.1	4.5	8,343.2	131.3	142.0	42.6
Q1 2003	2.1	4.6	1.1	4.0	5.9	4.2	1.2	2.9	4.2	6.5	5.8	4.3	8,051.9	134.1	148.0	34.7
Q2 2003	3.8	5.1	5.9	6.3	6.1	-0.7	1.0	2.6	3.8	5.7	5.5	4.2	9,342.4	137.0	149.0	29.1
Q3 2003	6.9	9.3	6.7	9.3	6.1	3.0	0.9	3.1	4.4	6.0	6.1	4.0	9,649.7	141.0	147.0	22.7
Q4 2003	4.8	6.8	1.6	3.3	5.8	1.5	0.9	3.2	4.4	5.8	5.9	4.0	10,799.6	145.9	146.0	21.1
Q1 2004	2.3	5.9	2.9	6.1	5.7	3.4	0.9	3.0	4.1	5.5	5.6	4.0	11,039.4	151.6	153.0	21.6
Q2 2004	3.0	6.6	4.0	7.0	5.6	3.2	1.1	3.7	4.7	6.1	6.2	4.0	11,144.6	157.9	160.0	20.0
Q3 2004	3.7	6.3	2.1	4.5	5.4	2.6	1.5	3.5	4.4	5.8	5.9	4.4	10,893.8	163.2	172.0	19.3
Q4 2004	3.5	6.4	5.1	8.5	5.4	4.4	2.0	3.5	4.3	5.4	5.7	4.9	11,951.5	169.2	176.0	16.6
Q1 2005	4.3	8.3	-3.8	-1.8	5.3	2.0	2.5	3.9	4.4	5.4	5.8	5.4	11,637.3	177.1	176.0	14.6
Q2 2005	2.1	5.1	3.2	6.0	5.1	2.7	2.9	3.9	4.2	5.5	5.7	5.9	11,856.7	184.5	182.0	17.7
Q3 2005	3.4	7.3	2.1	6.6	5.0	6.2	3.4	4.0	4.3	5.5	5.8	6.4	12,282.9	190.2	187.0	14.2
Q4 2005	2.3	5.4	3.4	6.6	5.0	3.8	3.8	4.4	4.6	5.9	6.2	7.0	12,497.2	194.8	195.0	16.5
Q1 2006	4.9	8.2	9.5	11.5	4.7	2.1	4.4	4.6	4.7	6.0	6.3	7.4	13,121.6	198.0	200.0	14.6
Q2 2006	1.2	4.5	0.6	3.7	4.6	3.7	4.7	5.0	5.2	6.5	6.6	7.9	12,808.9	197.1	209.0	23.8
Q3 2006	0.4	3.2	1.2	4.1	4.6	3.8	4.9	4.8	5.0	6.4	6.5	8.3	13,322.5	195.8	219.0	18.6
Q4 2006	3.2	4.6	5.3	4.6	4.4	-1.6	4.9	4.6	4.7	6.1	6.2	8.3	14,215.8	195.8	217.0	12.7
Q1 2007	0.2	4.8	2.6	6.5	4.5	4.0	5.0	4.6	4.8	6.1	6.2	8.3	14,354.0	193.3	227.0	19.6
Q2 2007	3.1	5.4	0.8	4.0	4.5	4.6	4.7	4.7	4.9	6.3	6.4	8.3	15,163.1	188.5	236.0	18.9
Q3 2007	2.7	4.2	1.1	3.4	4.7	2.6	4.3	4.5	4.8	6.5	6.5	8.2	15,317.8	183.2	249.0	30.8
Q4 2007	1.4	3.2	0.3	4.4	4.8	5.0	3.4	3.8	4.4	6.4	6.2	7.5	14,753.6	177.8	251.0	31.1
Q1 2008	-2.7	-0.5	2.9	6.5	5.0	4.4	2.1	2.8	3.9	6.5	5.9	6.2	13,284.1	171.1	240.0	32.2
Q2 2008	2.0	4.0	8.7	13.3	5.3	5.3	1.6	3.2	4.1	6.8	6.1	5.1	13,016.4	163.9	224.0	24.1
Q3 2008	-1.9	0.8	-8.9	-5.1	6.0	6.3	1.5	3.1	4.1	7.2	6.3	5.0	11,826.0	157.4	233.0	46.7
Q4 2008	-8.2	-7.7	2.6	-3.2	6.9	-8.9	0.3	2.2	3.7	9.4	5.8	4.1	9,056.7	149.5	223.0	80.9
Q1 2009	-5.4	-4.5	-0.8	-3.0	8.3	-2.7	0.2	1.9	3.2	9.0	5.0	3.3	8,044.2	143.5	209.0	56.7
Q2 2009	-0.5	-1.2	2.9	4.7	9.3	2.1	0.2	2.3	3.7	8.2	5.1	3.3	9,342.8	143.2	178.0	42.3
Q3 2009	1.3	1.2	-4.3	-1.9	9.6	3.5	0.2	2.5	3.8	6.8	5.1	3.3	10,812.8	144.3	154.0	31.3
Q4 2009	3.9	5.2	-0.5	2.2	9.9	3.2	0.1	2.3	3.7	6.1	4.9	3.3	11,385.1	145.2	155.0	30.7
Q1 2010	1.7	3.2	0.4	1.8	9.8	0.6	0.1	2.4	3.9	5.8	5.0	3.3	12,032.5	145.5	150.0	27.3
Q2 2010	3.9	5.8	5.3	5.8	9.6	-0.1	0.1	2.3	3.6	5.6	4.8	3.3	10,645.8	144.4	165.0	45.8
Q3 2010	2.7	4.6	2.0	3.2	9.5	1.2	0.2	1.6	2.9	5.1	4.4	3.3	11,814.0	141.6	167.0	32.9
Q4 2010	2.5	4.7	2.8	5.0	9.5	3.3	0.1	1.5	3.0	5.0	4.5	3.3	13,131.5	140.3	173.0	23.5
Q1 2011	-1.5	0.2	5.0	8.2	9.1	4.3	0.1	2.1	3.5	5.4	4.9	3.3	13,908.5	138.5	180.0	29.4
Q2 2011	2.9	6.0	-0.6	3.5	9.1	4.7	0.0	1.8	3.3	5.1	4.6	3.3	13,843.5	137.7	177.0	22.7
Q3 2011	0.8	3.3	2.1	4.3	9.0	2.6	0.0	1.1	2.5	4.9	4.2	3.3	11,676.5	137.7	177.0	48.0
Q4 2011	4.6	5.2	0.2	1.6	8.6	1.7	0.0	1.0	2.1	5.0	4.0	3.3	13,019.3	137.6	188.0	45.5
Q1 2012	2.7	4.9	6.7	9.2	8.3	2.2	0.1	0.9	2.1	4.7	3.9	3.3	14,627.5	139.6	188.0	23.0
Q2 2012	1.9	3.8	3.1	4.4	8.2	1.0	0.1	0.8	1.8	4.5	3.8	3.3	14,100.2	142.8	189.0	26.7
Q3 2012	0.5	2.7	-0.2	1.1	8.0	1.8	0.1	0.7	1.6	4.2	3.5	3.3	14,894.7	145.7	197.0	20.5
Q4 2012	0.1	1.7	10.9	13.3	7.8	2.6	0.1	0.7	1.7	3.9	3.4	3.3	14,834.9	149.3	198.0	22.7
Q1 2013	1.9	3.6	-15.9	-14.7	7.7	1.4	0.1	0.8	1.9	4.0	3.5	3.3	16,396.2	153.8	202.0	19.0
Q2 2013	1.1	2.1	2.7	3.1	7.5	-0.1	0.1	0.9	2.0	4.1	3.7	3.3	16,771.3	158.8	213.0	20.5
Q3 2013	3.0	4.9	2.2	3.9	7.2	2.3	0.0	1.5	2.7	4.9	4.4	3.3	17,718.3	163.0	224.0	17.0

(continued on next page)

Table 2A.— *continued*

Date	Real GDP growth	Nominal GDP growth	Real dispo-sable income growth	Nominal dispo-sable income growth	Unem-ployment rate	CPI inflation rate	3-month Treasury rate	5-year Treasury yield	10-year Treasury yield	BBB corporate yield	Mortgage rate	Prime rate	Level			
													Dow Jones Total Stock Market Index	House Price Index	Com-mercial Real Estate Price Index	Market Volatility Index
Q4 2013	3.8	5.6	0.6	2.0	7.0	1.4	0.1	1.4	2.8	4.8	4.3	3.3	19,413.2	166.3	229.0	20.3
Q1 2014	-0.9	0.6	4.0	5.6	6.7	2.1	0.0	1.6	2.8	4.6	4.4	3.3	19,711.2	169.3	230.0	21.4
Q2 2014	4.6	6.9	3.0	5.2	6.2	2.4	0.0	1.7	2.7	4.3	4.2	3.3	20,568.7	170.7	239.0	17.0
Q3 2014	4.3	6.0	2.7	3.9	6.1	1.2	0.0	1.7	2.5	4.2	4.1	3.3	20,458.8	172.5	245.0	17.0
Q4 2014	2.1	2.2	4.7	4.2	5.7	-0.9	0.0	1.6	2.3	4.2	3.9	3.3	21,424.6	174.5	252.0	26.3
Q1 2015	0.6	0.8	3.9	1.9	5.6	-3.1	0.0	1.5	2.0	4.0	3.7	3.3	21,707.6	177.3	260.0	22.4
Q2 2015	3.9	6.1	2.6	4.9	5.4	3.0	0.0	1.5	2.2	4.2	3.8	3.3	21,630.9	179.4	264.0	18.9
Q3 2015	2.0	3.3	3.8	5.1	5.2	1.6	0.0	1.6	2.3	4.5	3.9	3.3	19,959.3	181.7	270.0	40.7
Q4 2015	1.9	1.9	3.5	3.8	5.0	0.2	0.1	1.6	2.2	4.6	3.9	3.3	21,100.9	183.1	273.4	24.4
Q1 2016	-1.5	-0.1	2.3	1.2	5.5	-0.9	0.1	0.5	1.3	4.4	3.5	3.3	20,899.6	181.2	270.6	40.7
Q2 2016	-2.8	-3.0	0.3	-0.6	6.1	-0.7	0.1	0.7	1.4	4.9	3.8	3.3	18,454.3	178.7	264.2	37.0
Q3 2016	-2.0	-2.1	-0.2	-1.0	6.7	-0.5	0.1	0.8	1.5	5.1	4.0	3.3	16,692.8	175.9	257.7	38.4
Q4 2016	-1.1	-1.1	0.0	-0.3	7.1	-0.1	0.1	1.0	1.7	5.4	4.2	3.2	15,536.2	172.8	251.8	36.0
Q1 2017	0.0	0.2	0.9	1.0	7.4	0.3	0.1	1.2	1.8	5.4	4.3	3.2	15,745.4	169.8	246.6	32.0
Q2 2017	1.3	1.8	1.4	1.9	7.5	0.7	0.1	1.3	1.9	5.3	4.3	3.2	16,052.6	167.0	243.5	29.1
Q3 2017	1.7	2.6	1.1	1.9	7.5	1.0	0.1	1.5	2.2	5.4	4.5	3.2	16,396.9	164.5	240.5	26.8
Q4 2017	2.6	3.4	2.1	3.1	7.5	1.2	0.1	1.6	2.3	5.4	4.6	3.2	17,115.4	162.9	240.6	24.7
Q1 2018	2.6	3.4	2.3	3.4	7.4	1.3	0.1	1.8	2.4	5.4	4.7	3.2	17,806.7	161.7	241.0	23.1
Q2 2018	3.0	3.9	2.5	3.7	7.3	1.4	0.1	1.9	2.6	5.5	4.8	3.2	18,645.6	161.1	242.2	21.7
Q3 2018	3.0	4.0	2.6	3.8	7.2	1.5	0.1	2.1	2.8	5.5	4.9	3.2	19,184.9	161.0	244.4	21.0
Q4 2018	3.0	4.1	2.6	3.9	7.1	1.6	0.1	2.3	2.9	5.6	5.0	3.2	19,756.4	161.2	246.8	20.3
Q1 2019	3.0	4.2	2.4	3.9	7.0	1.7	0.1	2.4	3.0	5.6	5.1	3.2	20,341.0	161.6	249.4	19.8

Note: Refer to Notes Regarding Scenario Variables for more information on variables.

Table 2B. Supervisory adverse scenario: International, Q1:2001Q1:2019
Percent unless otherwise indicated

Date	Euro area real GDP growth	Euro area inflation	Euro area bilateral dollar exchange rate (USD/euro)	Developing Asia real GDP growth	Developing Asia inflation	Developing Asia bilateral dollar exchange rate (F/USD, index)	Japan real GDP growth	Japan inflation	Japan bilateral dollar exchange rate (yen/USD)	U.K. real GDP growth	U.K. inflation	U.K. bilateral dollar exchange rate (USD/pound)
Q1 2001	3.8	1.1	0.879	5.0	1.7	106.0	2.6	-1.2	125.5	4.6	0.1	1.419
Q2 2001	0.1	4.1	0.847	5.5	2.2	106.1	-0.7	-0.3	124.7	3.1	3.1	1.408
Q3 2001	0.3	1.4	0.910	4.7	1.1	106.4	-4.4	-1.1	119.2	2.6	1.0	1.469
Q4 2001	0.5	1.7	0.890	8.4	0.2	106.9	-0.5	-1.4	131.0	1.4	0.0	1.454
Q1 2002	0.9	3.0	0.872	7.6	0.4	107.3	-0.9	-2.7	132.7	1.6	1.9	1.425
Q2 2002	2.0	2.0	0.986	8.1	1.2	104.8	4.3	1.7	119.9	3.3	0.9	1.525
Q3 2002	1.6	1.6	0.988	7.3	1.3	105.5	2.6	-0.7	121.7	3.9	1.4	1.570
Q4 2002	0.3	2.4	1.049	6.4	0.9	104.5	1.5	-0.4	118.8	3.6	1.9	1.610
Q1 2003	-0.9	3.3	1.090	6.5	3.6	105.5	-2.2	-1.6	118.1	2.9	1.6	1.579
Q2 2003	0.4	0.3	1.150	2.3	1.2	104.0	5.2	1.7	119.9	3.7	0.3	1.653
Q3 2003	2.0	2.2	1.165	14.2	0.0	102.6	1.7	-0.7	111.4	3.1	1.7	1.662
Q4 2003	3.1	2.2	1.260	12.9	5.6	103.4	4.2	-0.6	107.1	3.0	1.7	1.784
Q1 2004	2.0	2.3	1.229	5.5	4.0	101.4	3.8	-0.9	104.2	2.7	1.3	1.840
Q2 2004	2.2	2.4	1.218	7.1	4.1	102.8	0.3	1.1	109.4	2.2	1.0	1.813
Q3 2004	1.3	2.0	1.242	8.2	3.9	102.7	0.6	0.1	110.2	0.9	1.1	1.809
Q4 2004	1.5	2.4	1.354	6.3	0.9	98.9	-1.0	1.7	102.7	1.9	2.4	1.916
Q1 2005	0.6	1.5	1.297	10.3	2.9	98.6	0.8	-2.7	107.2	2.8	2.6	1.889
Q2 2005	2.8	2.2	1.210	8.9	1.5	98.9	5.4	-1.2	110.9	4.4	1.9	1.793
Q3 2005	3.0	3.2	1.206	9.3	2.3	98.6	1.4	-1.3	113.3	4.1	2.7	1.770
Q4 2005	2.4	2.5	1.184	11.6	1.7	98.1	0.7	0.7	117.9	5.9	1.4	1.719
Q1 2006	3.7	1.7	1.214	10.9	2.4	96.8	1.7	1.3	117.5	1.5	1.9	1.739
Q2 2006	4.4	2.5	1.278	7.1	3.2	96.7	1.7	-0.1	114.5	1.2	3.0	1.849
Q3 2006	2.6	2.0	1.269	10.3	2.1	96.4	-0.3	0.5	118.0	0.5	3.3	1.872
Q4 2006	4.4	0.9	1.320	11.1	3.8	94.6	5.2	-0.4	119.0	2.3	2.6	1.959
Q1 2007	3.2	2.2	1.337	13.7	3.6	94.0	4.0	-0.2	117.6	3.9	2.6	1.969
Q2 2007	2.5	2.3	1.352	10.6	4.9	91.9	0.6	0.0	123.4	2.4	1.7	2.006
Q3 2007	2.0	2.1	1.422	8.6	7.4	90.6	-1.5	0.1	115.0	3.1	0.2	2.039
Q4 2007	2.0	4.9	1.460	12.9	6.1	89.4	3.4	2.2	111.7	3.1	4.0	1.984
Q1 2008	2.3	4.2	1.581	7.1	8.1	88.0	2.7	1.3	99.9	1.0	3.7	1.986
Q2 2008	-1.3	3.2	1.575	6.1	6.4	88.7	-4.6	1.6	106.2	-2.2	5.7	1.991
Q3 2008	-2.2	3.2	1.408	3.1	2.8	91.6	-4.1	3.6	105.9	-6.6	5.8	1.780
Q4 2008	-7.1	-1.4	1.392	0.1	-0.9	92.3	-12.5	-2.2	90.8	-8.7	0.5	1.462
Q1 2009	-11.3	-1.1	1.326	3.8	-1.4	94.2	-15.1	-3.6	99.2	-6.1	-0.1	1.430
Q2 2009	-0.8	0.0	1.402	15.4	2.3	92.3	7.1	-1.7	96.4	-0.8	2.2	1.645
Q3 2009	1.2	1.1	1.463	12.6	3.9	91.3	0.4	-1.2	89.5	0.6	3.5	1.600
Q4 2009	2.0	1.6	1.433	9.0	5.2	90.7	7.1	-1.6	93.1	1.4	3.0	1.617
Q1 2010	1.7	1.8	1.353	9.8	4.6	89.8	5.8	0.9	93.4	1.5	4.0	1.519
Q2 2010	3.9	2.0	1.229	9.8	3.4	91.1	4.6	-1.2	88.5	3.3	3.2	1.495
Q3 2010	1.9	1.6	1.360	8.8	3.9	88.4	6.1	-2.1	83.5	2.0	2.3	1.573
Q4 2010	2.1	2.6	1.327	9.3	7.7	87.4	-2.0	1.3	81.7	0.4	4.0	1.539
Q1 2011	3.5	3.6	1.418	9.5	6.3	86.5	-7.7	-0.4	82.8	3.0	6.7	1.605
Q2 2011	0.0	3.2	1.452	7.1	5.4	85.3	-2.2	-0.4	80.6	1.4	4.7	1.607
Q3 2011	-0.1	1.4	1.345	5.9	5.0	87.4	11.2	0.3	77.0	3.3	3.7	1.562
Q4 2011	-1.2	3.5	1.297	6.1	3.4	87.4	0.9	-0.7	77.0	0.6	3.4	1.554
Q1 2012	-0.7	2.7	1.333	7.1	3.2	86.4	3.6	1.9	82.4	0.9	2.1	1.599
Q2 2012	-1.3	2.3	1.267	5.9	4.0	88.1	-1.3	-0.7	79.8	-0.7	2.0	1.569
Q3 2012	-0.6	1.6	1.286	6.5	1.9	86.3	-1.9	-2.1	77.9	4.1	2.3	1.613
Q4 2012	-1.7	2.4	1.319	7.2	3.7	86.0	-0.4	0.0	86.6	-0.2	4.0	1.626
Q1 2013	-1.0	1.1	1.282	6.3	4.2	86.3	4.0	0.4	94.2	2.7	2.9	1.519
Q2 2013	1.6	0.5	1.301	7.0	3.1	87.3	3.1	0.6	99.2	2.4	1.7	1.521
Q3 2013	1.0	1.3	1.354	7.4	3.5	86.8	2.0	2.4	98.3	3.8	2.1	1.618

(continued on next page)

Table 2B.—*continued*

Date	Euro area real GDP growth	Euro area inflation	Euro area bilateral dollar exchange rate (USD/euro)	Developing Asia real GDP growth	Developing Asia inflation	Developing Asia bilateral dollar exchange rate (F/USD, index)	Japan real GDP growth	Japan inflation	Japan bilateral dollar exchange rate (yen/USD)	U.K. real GDP growth	U.K. inflation	U.K. bilateral dollar exchange rate (USD/pound)
Q4 2013	0.8	0.3	1.378	6.5	4.0	85.9	-0.7	2.3	105.3	2.6	1.5	1.657
Q1 2014	0.9	0.6	1.378	5.9	1.5	86.9	5.0	0.7	103.0	2.6	1.8	1.668
Q2 2014	0.2	0.1	1.369	7.0	2.7	86.8	-7.2	9.3	101.3	3.2	1.5	1.711
Q3 2014	1.2	0.3	1.263	7.5	2.2	87.2	-2.8	1.3	109.7	2.6	0.9	1.622
Q4 2014	1.5	-0.4	1.210	5.6	1.0	88.2	1.8	-0.8	119.9	2.7	-0.6	1.558
Q1 2015	2.2	-1.2	1.074	5.8	1.0	88.1	4.4	-0.3	120.0	1.5	-1.2	1.485
Q2 2015	1.6	2.2	1.115	6.2	2.9	88.5	-0.5	1.7	122.1	2.2	0.8	1.573
Q3 2015	1.2	-0.1	1.116	7.0	2.6	91.1	1.0	0.0	119.8	1.8	1.0	1.512
Q4 2015	1.6	-0.1	1.086	6.2	2.3	92.2	1.0	-0.3	120.3	2.4	-0.3	1.475
Q1 2016	-3.4	-0.5	0.991	-1.1	0.2	102.3	-4.0	-2.1	122.7	-2.1	-0.7	1.414
Q2 2016	-3.2	-0.8	0.982	0.4	-0.3	104.6	-5.7	-2.4	121.6	-2.6	-0.8	1.422
Q3 2016	-1.8	-0.6	0.976	3.8	-0.8	104.4	-5.0	-2.2	122.1	-1.9	-0.5	1.430
Q4 2016	-0.7	-0.3	0.972	5.5	-0.7	104.1	-3.8	-1.7	122.6	-0.9	-0.2	1.440
Q1 2017	0.2	0.1	0.981	6.2	-0.4	103.0	-2.8	-1.2	122.6	0.1	0.2	1.449
Q2 2017	0.9	0.4	0.991	6.3	-0.1	101.8	-1.9	-0.7	122.6	1.0	0.6	1.457
Q3 2017	1.5	0.6	1.000	6.3	0.3	100.6	-1.1	-0.4	122.6	1.7	0.8	1.464
Q4 2017	1.8	0.8	1.010	6.3	0.6	99.5	-0.3	-0.2	122.6	2.2	1.0	1.470
Q1 2018	2.0	0.9	1.019	6.3	0.8	98.6	0.4	-0.2	122.0	2.4	1.1	1.473
Q2 2018	2.1	1.0	1.027	6.4	1.1	97.8	0.9	-0.1	121.4	2.6	1.2	1.475
Q3 2018	2.1	1.1	1.035	6.5	1.4	97.1	1.2	0.0	120.8	2.7	1.3	1.477
Q4 2018	2.1	1.2	1.043	6.6	1.7	96.5	1.5	0.3	120.3	2.7	1.4	1.479
Q1 2019	2.0	1.3	1.051	6.7	2.0	96.1	1.6	0.6	119.4	2.7	1.5	1.484

Note: Refer to Notes Regarding Scenario Variables for more information on variables.

Table 3A. Supervisory severely adverse scenario: Domestic, Q1:2001Q1:2019
Percent unless otherwise indicated

Date	Real GDP growth	Nominal GDP growth	Real disposable income growth	Nominal disposable income growth	Unemployment rate	CPI inflation rate	3-month Treasury rate	5-year Treasury yield	10-year Treasury yield	BBB corporate yield	Mortgage rate	Prime rate	Dow Jones Total Stock Market Index	House Price Index	Commercial Real Estate Price Index	Market Volatility Index
													Level			
Q1 2001	-1.1	1.4	3.5	6.3	4.2	3.9	4.8	4.9	5.3	7.4	7.0	8.6	10,645.9	113.3	139.0	32.8
Q2 2001	2.1	5.1	-0.3	1.6	4.4	2.8	3.7	4.9	5.5	7.5	7.1	7.3	11,407.2	115.2	139.0	34.7
Q3 2001	-1.3	0.0	9.8	10.1	4.8	1.1	3.2	4.6	5.3	7.3	6.9	6.6	9,563.0	117.5	141.0	43.7
Q4 2001	1.1	2.3	-4.9	-4.6	5.5	-0.3	1.9	4.2	5.1	7.2	6.8	5.2	10,707.7	119.8	136.0	35.3
Q1 2002	3.7	5.1	10.1	10.9	5.7	1.3	1.7	4.5	5.4	7.6	7.0	4.8	10,775.7	122.1	137.0	26.1
Q2 2002	2.2	3.8	2.0	5.2	5.8	3.2	1.7	4.5	5.4	7.6	6.8	4.8	9,384.0	125.4	136.0	28.4
Q3 2002	2.0	3.8	-0.5	1.5	5.7	2.2	1.6	3.4	4.5	7.3	6.2	4.8	7,773.6	128.6	139.0	45.1
Q4 2002	0.3	2.4	1.9	3.8	5.9	2.4	1.3	3.1	4.3	7.0	6.1	4.5	8,343.2	131.3	142.0	42.6
Q1 2003	2.1	4.6	1.1	4.0	5.9	4.2	1.2	2.9	4.2	6.5	5.8	4.3	8,051.9	134.1	148.0	34.7
Q2 2003	3.8	5.1	5.9	6.3	6.1	-0.7	1.0	2.6	3.8	5.7	5.5	4.2	9,342.4	137.0	149.0	29.1
Q3 2003	6.9	9.3	6.7	9.3	6.1	3.0	0.9	3.1	4.4	6.0	6.1	4.0	9,649.7	141.0	147.0	22.7
Q4 2003	4.8	6.8	1.6	3.3	5.8	1.5	0.9	3.2	4.4	5.8	5.9	4.0	10,799.6	145.9	146.0	21.1
Q1 2004	2.3	5.9	2.9	6.1	5.7	3.4	0.9	3.0	4.1	5.5	5.6	4.0	11,039.4	151.6	153.0	21.6
Q2 2004	3.0	6.6	4.0	7.0	5.6	3.2	1.1	3.7	4.7	6.1	6.2	4.0	11,144.6	157.9	160.0	20.0
Q3 2004	3.7	6.3	2.1	4.5	5.4	2.6	1.5	3.5	4.4	5.8	5.9	4.4	10,893.8	163.2	172.0	19.3
Q4 2004	3.5	6.4	5.1	8.5	5.4	4.4	2.0	3.5	4.3	5.4	5.7	4.9	11,951.5	169.2	176.0	16.6
Q1 2005	4.3	8.3	-3.8	-1.8	5.3	2.0	2.5	3.9	4.4	5.4	5.8	5.4	11,637.3	177.1	176.0	14.6
Q2 2005	2.1	5.1	3.2	6.0	5.1	2.7	2.9	3.9	4.2	5.5	5.7	5.9	11,856.7	184.5	182.0	17.7
Q3 2005	3.4	7.3	2.1	6.6	5.0	6.2	3.4	4.0	4.3	5.5	5.8	6.4	12,282.9	190.2	187.0	14.2
Q4 2005	2.3	5.4	3.4	6.6	5.0	3.8	3.8	4.4	4.6	5.9	6.2	7.0	12,497.2	194.8	195.0	16.5
Q1 2006	4.9	8.2	9.5	11.5	4.7	2.1	4.4	4.6	4.7	6.0	6.3	7.4	13,121.6	198.0	200.0	14.6
Q2 2006	1.2	4.5	0.6	3.7	4.6	3.7	4.7	5.0	5.2	6.5	6.6	7.9	12,808.9	197.1	209.0	23.8
Q3 2006	0.4	3.2	1.2	4.1	4.6	3.8	4.9	4.8	5.0	6.4	6.5	8.3	13,322.5	195.8	219.0	18.6
Q4 2006	3.2	4.6	5.3	4.6	4.4	-1.6	4.9	4.6	4.7	6.1	6.2	8.3	14,215.8	195.8	217.0	12.7
Q1 2007	0.2	4.8	2.6	6.5	4.5	4.0	5.0	4.6	4.8	6.1	6.2	8.3	14,354.0	193.3	227.0	19.6
Q2 2007	3.1	5.4	0.8	4.0	4.5	4.6	4.7	4.7	4.9	6.3	6.4	8.3	15,163.1	188.5	236.0	18.9
Q3 2007	2.7	4.2	1.1	3.4	4.7	2.6	4.3	4.5	4.8	6.5	6.5	8.2	15,317.8	183.2	249.0	30.8
Q4 2007	1.4	3.2	0.3	4.4	4.8	5.0	3.4	3.8	4.4	6.4	6.2	7.5	14,753.6	177.8	251.0	31.1
Q1 2008	-2.7	-0.5	2.9	6.5	5.0	4.4	2.1	2.8	3.9	6.5	5.9	6.2	13,284.1	171.1	240.0	32.2
Q2 2008	2.0	4.0	8.7	13.3	5.3	5.3	1.6	3.2	4.1	6.8	6.1	5.1	13,016.4	163.9	224.0	24.1
Q3 2008	-1.9	0.8	-8.9	-5.1	6.0	6.3	1.5	3.1	4.1	7.2	6.3	5.0	11,826.0	157.4	233.0	46.7
Q4 2008	-8.2	-7.7	2.6	-3.2	6.9	-8.9	0.3	2.2	3.7	9.4	5.8	4.1	9,056.7	149.5	223.0	80.9
Q1 2009	-5.4	-4.5	-0.8	-3.0	8.3	-2.7	0.2	1.9	3.2	9.0	5.0	3.3	8,044.2	143.5	209.0	56.7
Q2 2009	-0.5	-1.2	2.9	4.7	9.3	2.1	0.2	2.3	3.7	8.2	5.1	3.3	9,342.8	143.2	178.0	42.3
Q3 2009	1.3	1.2	-4.3	-1.9	9.6	3.5	0.2	2.5	3.8	6.8	5.1	3.3	10,812.8	144.3	154.0	31.3
Q4 2009	3.9	5.2	-0.5	2.2	9.9	3.2	0.1	2.3	3.7	6.1	4.9	3.3	11,385.1	145.2	155.0	30.7
Q1 2010	1.7	3.2	0.4	1.8	9.8	0.6	0.1	2.4	3.9	5.8	5.0	3.3	12,032.5	145.5	150.0	27.3
Q2 2010	3.9	5.8	5.3	5.8	9.6	-0.1	0.1	2.3	3.6	5.6	4.8	3.3	10,645.8	144.4	165.0	45.8
Q3 2010	2.7	4.6	2.0	3.2	9.5	1.2	0.2	1.6	2.9	5.1	4.4	3.3	11,814.0	141.6	167.0	32.9
Q4 2010	2.5	4.7	2.8	5.0	9.5	3.3	0.1	1.5	3.0	5.0	4.5	3.3	13,131.5	140.3	173.0	23.5
Q1 2011	-1.5	0.2	5.0	8.2	9.1	4.3	0.1	2.1	3.5	5.4	4.9	3.3	13,908.5	138.5	180.0	29.4
Q2 2011	2.9	6.0	-0.6	3.5	9.1	4.7	0.0	1.8	3.3	5.1	4.6	3.3	13,843.5	137.7	177.0	22.7
Q3 2011	0.8	3.3	2.1	4.3	9.0	2.6	0.0	1.1	2.5	4.9	4.2	3.3	11,676.5	137.7	177.0	48.0
Q4 2011	4.6	5.2	0.2	1.6	8.6	1.7	0.0	1.0	2.1	5.0	4.0	3.3	13,019.3	137.6	188.0	45.5
Q1 2012	2.7	4.9	6.7	9.2	8.3	2.2	0.1	0.9	2.1	4.7	3.9	3.3	14,627.5	139.6	188.0	23.0
Q2 2012	1.9	3.8	3.1	4.4	8.2	1.0	0.1	0.8	1.8	4.5	3.8	3.3	14,100.2	142.8	189.0	26.7
Q3 2012	0.5	2.7	-0.2	1.1	8.0	1.8	0.1	0.7	1.6	4.2	3.5	3.3	14,894.7	145.7	197.0	20.5
Q4 2012	0.1	1.7	10.9	13.3	7.8	2.6	0.1	0.7	1.7	3.9	3.4	3.3	14,834.9	149.3	198.0	22.7
Q1 2013	1.9	3.6	-15.9	-14.7	7.7	1.4	0.1	0.8	1.9	4.0	3.5	3.3	16,396.2	153.8	202.0	19.0
Q2 2013	1.1	2.1	2.7	3.1	7.5	-0.1	0.1	0.9	2.0	4.1	3.7	3.3	16,771.3	158.8	213.0	20.5
Q3 2013	3.0	4.9	2.2	3.9	7.2	2.3	0.0	1.5	2.7	4.9	4.4	3.3	17,718.3	163.0	224.0	17.0

(continued on next page)

Table 3A.—*continued*

Date	Real GDP growth	Nominal GDP growth	Real disposable income growth	Nominal disposable income growth	Unemployment rate	CPI inflation rate	3-month Treasury rate	5-year Treasury yield	10-year Treasury yield	BBB corporate yield	Mortgage rate	Prime rate	Level			
													Dow Jones Total Stock Market Index	House Price Index	Commercial Real Estate Price Index	Market Volatility Index
Q4 2013	3.8	5.6	0.6	2.0	7.0	1.4	0.1	1.4	2.8	4.8	4.3	3.3	19,413.2	166.3	229.0	20.3
Q1 2014	-0.9	0.6	4.0	5.6	6.7	2.1	0.0	1.6	2.8	4.6	4.4	3.3	19,711.2	169.3	230.0	21.4
Q2 2014	4.6	6.9	3.0	5.2	6.2	2.4	0.0	1.7	2.7	4.3	4.2	3.3	20,568.7	170.7	239.0	17.0
Q3 2014	4.3	6.0	2.7	3.9	6.1	1.2	0.0	1.7	2.5	4.2	4.1	3.3	20,458.8	172.5	245.0	17.0
Q4 2014	2.1	2.2	4.7	4.2	5.7	-0.9	0.0	1.6	2.3	4.2	3.9	3.3	21,424.6	174.5	252.0	26.3
Q1 2015	0.6	0.8	3.9	1.9	5.6	-3.1	0.0	1.5	2.0	4.0	3.7	3.3	21,707.6	177.3	260.0	22.4
Q2 2015	3.9	6.1	2.6	4.9	5.4	3.0	0.0	1.5	2.2	4.2	3.8	3.3	21,630.9	179.4	264.0	18.9
Q3 2015	2.0	3.3	3.8	5.1	5.2	1.6	0.0	1.6	2.3	4.5	3.9	3.3	19,959.3	181.7	270.0	40.7
Q4 2015	1.9	1.9	3.5	3.8	5.0	0.2	0.1	1.6	2.2	4.6	3.9	3.3	21,100.9	183.1	273.4	24.4
Q1 2016	-5.1	-2.6	-0.5	-0.4	6.0	0.2	0.0	0.0	0.2	4.8	3.2	3.3	16,831.9	178.8	264.9	73.3
Q2 2016	-7.5	-6.1	-4.1	-3.2	7.2	0.9	-0.2	0.0	0.4	5.6	3.7	2.9	13,254.9	173.5	251.0	61.1
Q3 2016	-5.9	-4.5	-4.5	-3.5	8.3	1.1	-0.5	0.0	0.4	6.0	3.9	2.6	11,469.2	167.4	236.5	67.1
Q4 2016	-4.2	-2.9	-3.6	-2.5	9.1	1.3	-0.5	0.0	0.6	6.4	4.1	2.6	10,395.5	160.8	223.2	59.1
Q1 2017	-2.2	-0.9	-2.0	-0.7	9.7	1.4	-0.5	0.0	0.7	6.1	4.1	2.6	11,183.3	154.7	210.4	45.5
Q2 2017	0.4	1.9	-0.7	1.0	9.9	1.8	-0.5	0.0	0.8	5.8	4.1	2.6	12,131.9	148.9	201.3	37.4
Q3 2017	1.3	2.9	-0.3	1.4	10.0	1.9	-0.5	0.1	1.0	5.7	4.1	2.6	13,178.9	144.0	193.4	31.1
Q4 2017	3.0	4.4	1.4	3.1	9.9	1.9	-0.5	0.2	1.1	5.5	4.1	2.6	14,671.1	140.8	191.2	26.2
Q1 2018	3.0	4.0	2.3	3.6	9.8	1.6	-0.5	0.3	1.2	5.3	4.1	2.6	16,180.1	138.5	190.1	22.8
Q2 2018	3.9	5.0	2.6	4.0	9.6	1.7	-0.5	0.4	1.4	5.1	4.0	2.6	17,996.1	137.5	190.5	20.0
Q3 2018	3.9	4.9	2.9	4.3	9.4	1.7	0.5	0.5	1.5	5.0	4.1	2.6	19,271.6	137.3	192.6	18.9
Q4 2018	3.9	4.9	3.1	4.4	9.1	1.6	-0.5	0.6	1.6	4.8	4.1	2.6	20,640.9	137.7	195.4	17.6
Q1 2019	3.9	4.8	3.0	4.2	8.9	1.5	-0.5	0.7	1.7	4.7	4.1	2.6	22,068.1	138.5	198.5	16.8

Note: Refer to Notes Regarding Scenario Variables for more information on variables.

Table 3B. Supervisory severely adverse scenario: International, Q1:2001Q1:2019
Percent unless otherwise indicated

Date	Euro area real GDP growth	Euro area inflation	Euro area bilateral dollar exchange rate (USD/euro)	Developing Asia real GDP growth	Developing Asia inflation	Developing Asia bilateral dollar exchange rate (F/USD, index)	Japan real GDP growth	Japan inflation	Japan bilateral dollar exchange rate (yen/USD)	U.K. real GDP growth	U.K. inflation	U.K. bilateral dollar exchange rate (USD/pound)
Q1 2001	3.8	1.1	0.879	5.0	1.7	106.0	2.6	-1.2	125.5	4.6	0.1	1.419
Q2 2001	0.1	4.1	0.847	5.5	2.2	106.1	-0.7	-0.3	124.7	3.1	3.1	1.408
Q3 2001	0.3	1.4	0.910	4.7	1.1	106.4	-4.4	-1.1	119.2	2.6	1.0	1.469
Q4 2001	0.5	1.7	0.890	8.4	0.2	106.9	-0.5	-1.4	131.0	1.4	0.0	1.454
Q1 2002	0.9	3.0	0.872	7.6	0.4	107.3	-0.9	-2.7	132.7	1.6	1.9	1.425
Q2 2002	2.0	2.0	0.986	8.1	1.2	104.8	4.3	1.7	119.9	3.3	0.9	1.525
Q3 2002	1.6	1.6	0.988	7.3	1.3	105.5	2.6	-0.7	121.7	3.9	1.4	1.570
Q4 2002	0.3	2.4	1.049	6.4	0.9	104.5	1.5	-0.4	118.8	3.6	1.9	1.610
Q1 2003	-0.9	3.3	1.090	6.5	3.6	105.5	-2.2	-1.6	118.1	2.9	1.6	1.579
Q2 2003	0.4	0.3	1.150	2.3	1.2	104.0	5.2	1.7	119.9	3.7	0.3	1.653
Q3 2003	2.0	2.2	1.165	14.2	0.0	102.6	1.7	-0.7	111.4	3.1	1.7	1.662
Q4 2003	3.1	2.2	1.260	12.9	5.6	103.4	4.2	-0.6	107.1	3.0	1.7	1.784
Q1 2004	2.0	2.3	1.229	5.5	4.0	101.4	3.8	-0.9	104.2	2.7	1.3	1.840
Q2 2004	2.2	2.4	1.218	7.1	4.1	102.8	0.3	1.1	109.4	2.2	1.0	1.813
Q3 2004	1.3	2.0	1.242	8.2	3.9	102.7	0.6	0.1	110.2	0.9	1.1	1.809
Q4 2004	1.5	2.4	1.354	6.3	0.9	98.9	-1.0	1.7	102.7	1.9	2.4	1.916
Q1 2005	0.6	1.5	1.297	10.3	2.9	98.6	0.8	-2.7	107.2	2.8	2.6	1.889
Q2 2005	2.8	2.2	1.210	8.9	1.5	98.9	5.4	-1.2	110.9	4.4	1.9	1.793
Q3 2005	3.0	3.2	1.206	9.3	2.3	98.6	1.4	-1.3	113.3	4.1	2.7	1.770
Q4 2005	2.4	2.5	1.184	11.6	1.7	98.1	0.7	0.7	117.9	5.9	1.4	1.719
Q1 2006	3.7	1.7	1.214	10.9	2.4	96.8	1.7	1.3	117.5	1.5	1.9	1.739
Q2 2006	4.4	2.5	1.278	7.1	3.2	96.7	1.7	-0.1	114.5	1.2	3.0	1.849
Q3 2006	2.6	2.0	1.269	10.3	2.1	96.4	-0.3	0.5	118.0	0.5	3.3	1.872
Q4 2006	4.4	0.9	1.320	11.1	3.8	94.6	5.2	-0.4	119.0	2.3	2.6	1.959
Q1 2007	3.2	2.2	1.337	13.7	3.6	94.0	4.0	-0.2	117.6	3.9	2.6	1.969
Q2 2007	2.5	2.3	1.352	10.6	4.9	91.9	0.6	0.0	123.4	2.4	1.7	2.006
Q3 2007	2.0	2.1	1.422	8.6	7.4	90.6	-1.5	0.1	115.0	3.1	0.2	2.039
Q4 2007	2.0	4.9	1.460	12.9	6.1	89.4	3.4	2.2	111.7	3.1	4.0	1.984
Q1 2008	2.3	4.2	1.581	7.1	8.1	88.0	2.7	1.3	99.9	1.0	3.7	1.986
Q2 2008	-1.3	3.2	1.575	6.1	6.4	88.7	-4.6	1.6	106.2	-2.2	5.7	1.991
Q3 2008	-2.2	3.2	1.408	3.1	2.8	91.6	-4.1	3.6	105.9	-6.6	5.8	1.780
Q4 2008	-7.1	-1.4	1.392	0.1	-0.9	92.3	-12.5	-2.2	90.8	-8.7	0.5	1.462
Q1 2009	-11.3	-1.1	1.326	3.8	-1.4	94.2	-15.1	-3.6	99.2	-6.1	-0.1	1.430
Q2 2009	-0.8	0.0	1.402	15.4	2.3	92.3	7.1	-1.7	96.4	-0.8	2.2	1.645
Q3 2009	1.2	1.1	1.463	12.6	3.9	91.3	0.4	-1.2	89.5	0.6	3.5	1.600
Q4 2009	2.0	1.6	1.433	9.0	5.2	90.7	7.1	-1.6	93.1	1.4	3.0	1.617
Q1 2010	1.7	1.8	1.353	9.8	4.6	89.8	5.8	0.9	93.4	1.5	4.0	1.519
Q2 2010	3.9	2.0	1.229	9.8	3.4	91.1	4.6	-1.2	88.5	3.3	3.2	1.495
Q3 2010	1.9	1.6	1.360	8.8	3.9	88.4	6.1	-2.1	83.5	2.0	2.3	1.573
Q4 2010	2.1	2.6	1.327	9.3	7.7	87.4	-2.0	1.3	81.7	0.4	4.0	1.539
Q1 2011	3.5	3.6	1.418	9.5	6.3	86.5	-7.7	-0.4	82.8	3.0	6.7	1.605
Q2 2011	0.0	3.2	1.452	7.1	5.4	85.3	-2.2	-0.4	80.6	1.4	4.7	1.607
Q3 2011	-0.1	1.4	1.345	5.9	5.0	87.4	11.2	0.3	77.0	3.3	3.7	1.562
Q4 2011	-1.2	3.5	1.297	6.1	3.4	87.4	0.9	-0.7	77.0	0.6	3.4	1.554
Q1 2012	-0.7	2.7	1.333	7.1	3.2	86.4	3.6	1.9	82.4	0.9	2.1	1.599
Q2 2012	-1.3	2.3	1.267	5.9	4.0	88.1	-1.3	-0.7	79.8	-0.7	2.0	1.569
Q3 2012	-0.6	1.6	1.286	6.5	1.9	86.3	-1.9	-2.1	77.9	4.1	2.3	1.613
Q4 2012	-1.7	2.4	1.319	7.2	3.7	86.0	-0.4	0.0	86.6	-0.2	4.0	1.626
Q1 2013	-1.0	1.1	1.282	6.3	4.2	86.3	4.0	0.4	94.2	2.7	2.9	1.519
Q2 2013	1.6	0.5	1.301	7.0	3.1	87.3	3.1	0.6	99.2	2.4	1.7	1.521
Q3 2013	1.0	1.3	1.354	7.4	3.5	86.8	2.0	2.4	98.3	3.8	2.1	1.618

(continued on next page)

Table 3B.—continued

Date	Euro area real GDP growth	Euro area inflation	Euro area bilateral dollar exchange rate (USD/euro)	Developing Asia real GDP growth	Developing Asia inflation	Developing Asia bilateral dollar exchange rate (F/USD, index)	Japan real GDP growth	Japan inflation	Japan bilateral dollar exchange rate (yen/USD)	U.K. real GDP growth	U.K. inflation	U.K. bilateral dollar exchange rate (USD/pound)
Q4 2013	0.8	0.3	1.378	6.5	4.0	85.9	-0.7	2.3	105.3	2.6	1.5	1.657
Q1 2014	0.9	0.6	1.378	5.9	1.5	86.9	5.0	0.7	103.0	2.6	1.8	1.668
Q2 2014	0.2	0.1	1.369	7.0	2.7	86.8	-7.2	9.3	101.3	3.2	1.5	1.711
Q3 2014	1.2	0.3	1.263	7.5	2.2	87.2	-2.8	1.3	109.7	2.6	0.9	1.622
Q4 2014	1.5	-0.4	1.210	5.6	1.0	88.2	1.8	-0.8	119.9	2.7	-0.6	1.558
Q1 2015	2.2	-1.2	1.074	5.8	1.0	88.1	4.4	-0.3	120.0	1.5	-1.2	1.485
Q2 2015	1.6	2.2	1.115	6.2	2.9	88.5	-0.5	1.7	122.1	2.2	0.8	1.573
Q3 2015	1.2	-0.1	1.116	7.0	2.6	91.1	1.0	0.0	119.8	1.8	1.0	1.512
Q4 2015	1.6	-0.1	1.086	6.2	2.3	92.2	1.0	-0.3	120.3	2.4	-0.3	1.475
Q1 2016	-4.4	-0.4	1.002	-1.4	0.1	100.9	-4.1	-2.8	117.0	-2.6	-0.8	1.439
Q2 2016	-5.4	-1.0	0.970	-0.8	-1.1	105.0	-7.5	-3.7	115.5	-4.4	-1.3	1.425
Q3 2016	-4.4	-1.3	0.952	1.5	-1.9	107.2	-9.0	-4.3	114.9	-4.1	-1.4	1.422
Q4 2016	-3.4	-1.2	0.935	2.9	-2.4	108.7	-9.6	-4.6	114.2	-3.4	-1.3	1.418
Q1 2017	-1.6	-0.9	0.946	5.0	-2.2	107.1	-8.1	-3.8	114.2	-1.9	-0.9	1.428
Q2 2017	-0.2	-0.5	0.957	6.1	-1.9	105.3	-6.0	-3.1	114.2	-0.4	-0.4	1.438
Q3 2017	0.9	-0.1	0.968	6.4	-1.4	103.5	-4.1	-2.5	114.3	0.8	0.0	1.446
Q4 2017	1.6	0.2	0.979	6.5	-1.0	101.9	-2.4	-2.1	114.3	1.7	0.3	1.453
Q1 2018	2.1	0.4	0.989	6.5	-0.5	100.5	-1.0	-1.7	113.8	2.3	0.6	1.456
Q2 2018	2.3	0.6	0.999	6.6	-0.1	99.2	0.1	-1.4	113.4	2.7	0.8	1.457
Q3 2018	2.4	0.7	1.009	6.7	0.3	98.1	0.9	-1.1	113.1	3.0	1.0	1.459
Q4 2018	2.4	0.9	1.018	6.8	0.8	97.3	1.4	-0.7	112.7	3.1	1.1	1.461
Q1 2019	2.3	1.0	1.028	7.0	1.2	96.5	1.7	-0.2	112.1	3.1	1.3	1.466

Note: Refer to Notes Regarding Scenario Variables for more information on variables.

Notes Regarding Scenario Variables

Sources for data through 2015:Q4 (as released through 1/20/2016). The 2015:Q4 values of variables marked with an asterisk (*) are projected.

*U.S. real GDP growth: Percent change in real gross domestic product at an annualized rate, Bureau of Economic Analysis.

*U.S. nominal GDP growth: Percent change in nominal gross domestic product at an annualized rate, Bureau of Economic Analysis.

*U.S. real disposable income growth: Percent change in nominal disposable personal income divided by the price index for personal consumption expenditures at an annualized rate, Bureau of Economic Analysis.

*U.S. nominal disposable income growth: Percent change in nominal disposable personal income at an annualized rate, Bureau of Economic Analysis.

U.S. unemployment rate: Quarterly average of monthly data, Bureau of Labor Statistics.

U.S. CPI inflation: Percent change in the quarterly average of the consumer price index at an annualized rate, Bureau of Labor Statistics.

U.S. 3-month Treasury rate: Quarterly average of 3-month Treasury bill secondary market rate on a discount basis, H.15 Release, Selected Interest Rates, Federal Reserve Board.

U.S. 5-year Treasury yield: Quarterly average of the yield on 5-year U.S. Treasury bonds, constructed for the FRB/U.S. model by Federal Reserve staff based on the Svensson smoothed term structure model; see Lars E. O. Svensson (1995), "Estimating Forward Interest Rates with the Extended Nelson-Siegel Method," *Quarterly Review*, no. 3, Sveriges Riksbank, pp. 13–26.

U.S. 10-year Treasury yield: Quarterly average of the yield on 10-year U.S. Treasury bonds, constructed for the FRB/U.S. model by Federal Reserve staff based on the Svensson smoothed term structure model; see id.

U.S. BBB corporate yield: Quarterly average of the yield on 10-year BBB-rated corporate bonds, constructed for the FRB/U.S. model by Federal Reserve staff using a Nelson-Siegel smoothed yield curve model; see Charles R. Nelson and Andrew F. Siegel (1987), "Parsimonious Modeling of Yield Curves," *Journal of Business*, vol. 60, pp. 473–89). Data prior to 1997 is based on the WARGA database. Data after 1997 is based on the Merrill Lynch database.

U.S. mortgage rate: Quarterly average of weekly series for the interest rate of a conventional, conforming, 30-year fixed-rate mortgage, obtained from the Primary Mortgage Market Survey of the Federal Home Loan Mortgage Corporation.

U.S. prime rate: Quarterly average of monthly series, H.15 Release, Selected Interest Rates, Federal Reserve Board.

U.S. Dow Jones Total Stock Market (Float Cap) Index: End of quarter value, Dow Jones.

*****U.S. House Price Index:** CoreLogic, index level, seasonally adjusted by Federal Reserve staff.

*****U.S. Commercial Real Estate Price Index:** From the Financial Accounts of the United States, Federal Reserve Board (Z.1 release); the series corresponds to the data for price indexes: Commercial Real Estate Price Index (series FL075035503.Q divided by 1000).

U.S. Market Volatility Index (VIX): Chicago Board Options Exchange, converted to quarterly by using the maximum close-of-day value in any quarter.

*****Euro area real GDP growth:** Percent change in real gross domestic product at an annualized rate, staff calculations based on Statistical Office of the European Communities via Haver, extended back using ECB Area Wide Model dataset (ECB Working Paper series no. 42).

Euro area inflation: Percent change in the quarterly average of the harmonized index of consumer prices at an annualized rate, staff calculations based on Statistical Office of the European Communities via Haver.

*****Developing Asia real GDP growth:** Percent change in real gross domestic product at an annualized rate, staff calculations based on Bank of Korea via Haver; Chinese National Bureau of Statistics via CEIC; Indian Central Statistical Organization via CEIC; Census and Statistics Department of Hong Kong via CEIC; and Taiwan Directorate-General of Budget, Accounting, and Statistics via CEIC.

*****Developing Asia inflation:** Percent change in the quarterly average of the consumer price index, or local equivalent, at an annualized rate, staff calculations based on Chinese National Bureau of Statistics via CEIC; Indian Ministry of Statistics and Programme Implementation via Haver; Labour Bureau of India via CEIC; National Statistical Office of Korea via CEIC; Census and Statistic Department of Hong Kong via CEIC; and Taiwan Directorate-General of Budget, Accounting, and Statistics via CEIC.

*****Japan real GDP growth:** Percent change in gross domestic product at an annualized rate, Cabinet Office via Haver.

*****Japan inflation:** Percent change in the quarterly average of the consumer price index at an annualized rate, Ministry of Internal Affairs and Communications via Haver.

*****U.K. real GDP growth:** Percent change in gross domestic product at an annualized rate, Office for National Statistics via Haver.

U.K. inflation: Percent change in the quarterly average of the consumer price index at an annualized rate, Office for National Statistics via Haver.

Exchange rates: Quarterly average of daily rates, Bloomberg.